Landscape or Land?

poems for Devon

Mark Beeson

Christopher Southgate

for Bobbie

with love

Mark

First published in Great Britain in 1989 by :

Wheal Press, Easdon Farm, Manaton, Newton Abbot, Devon.

Acknowledgements :

Some of these poems formed part of Christopher Southgate's pamphlet Annotations, which won an Iolaire Arts Prize in 1987 - that collection to be published by Aquila Press.

Some of these poems have appeared in the following magazines :

Envoi, Nexus, Otter, The PEN, Prospice, Westwords.

Cover : detail from a mural by Dickon Fell.

Printed by St Michael's Press, Pinhoe, Exeter, Devon.

Bound by Eric Gray, Bookbinder, Silverton, Exeter, Devon.

British Library Cataloguing in Publication Data

Beeson, Mark

Landscape or Land? : poems for Devon.
I. Title II. Southgate, Christopher, 1953-
821'.914

ISBN 0-9511588-1-3

CONTENTS

******

TWENTY-THREE POEMS BY MARK BEESON

The Home Range

I

Continent-roaming, made in England,
The Land Rover fills Malawi air
With the blue scorch of its gear ratios.
'Do you mean to say,' somebody asks
'There's a group inhabits that patch of
Forest you could fit in your pocket?'
'I do,' I say, and never divulge
How large it is, how day after day
I would search for the monkeys through it,
Hear them, and yet not once catch a glimpse
Of their blue flanks among its green clouds.

II

As I lay down on Zomba mountain,
I heard a voice crying in the dark;
A coughing cry, harsh, terrible
Whose only word was plain and stark:

Go. At night on Zomba mountain
Rain drummed down on the tin roof;
Creosote stained the air with harshness;
A leopard coughed across the kloof.

Darkness, darkness, all was darkness,
Black and terrible, harsh and plain -
Saying to me 'Sunshine, hey white man!
Time is up for you. Home again.'

On What Deep Chord

On what deep chord, depressed by the past
And silent now, does it resonate?
On what arch pattern of history
Does it find its template, that feeling
Of communion, experience
Of unity, love of two people
Looking at the same light together
From dimness, and those scents which join me
To memory in the veins of lanes
Where my heart is? On some huge empire?
On a single person, one as small
As you or me, and in a slim province
Hard to distinguish on the blue globes
We spin at home imperiously.

Against Taking Holidays Away

I don't believe in going away
When I've been given a holiday.
Holy days are for holier things:
Pushing a child on the playground swings,
Looking for visions down the garden.
Little could make my feelings harden
(To people I haven't a grouse with) more
Than knowing their car has come on tour.
They're foreign to me, they don't belong,
They're not even friends of friends along.
They terrorise me when I'm at large
With a bike or pushchair in my charge.
It terrifies me the way they go
Too fast down a lane they don't yet know.
I don't think I'd want to do the same
To them in the place from where they came,
Don't think I'd want to look at them, too,
As if they were in some kind of zoo
Like they wind up their windows at me
As a local curiosity.
Holy days are for holier thoughts
Than 'wish-you-were-here's from sun resorts.
As for the heat, I've begun to learn
Back-yard bushes are the ones which burn.
Yes, if I'm going to visit friends,
And yes again if it's work that sends
Me off; the gift, though, of holiday
Is time I don't want taken away.

The Spectre of Spectator Sport

The fledgling swallow with its siblings
Crouched on the wire, precariously,
Will only have to watch its parents
Some short period from a distance,
Catching or failing to catch it food
As they slalom the fly-rich breezes.
We, though, have plumped for a life of it.
To watch, on screen, our sporting heroes
Induces helplessness of the worst
Possible kind. Nothing you can do
Has any influence. If they win,
It isn't because of your hard work
Encouraging them, and, easy-won,
The ecstasy is ephemeral.
If they should lose, on the other hand,
No misery is more depressing
Because of its making you aware
Just how little you are in control,
Any longer, of your happiness.
Sport should be local to those who watch
And the heroes known to have clay feet
And to be more than amenable
To the odd word of advice, the odd
Term of abuse with their accolades;
To be a son or sister-in-law
Or a friend we have been to school with -
What happens on an undulating
Cricket pitch that is grazed all winter
Beneath Chagford, or a tennis court
Built with parish funds in Widecombe,
More live to us than the tiny ghosts
Of Lord's and Wimbledon which flicker
On hot, neglected summer afternoons
In the shadowy tombs of parlours.

Lacking a Scent

I went to Oxford and ached my days
At the unrecognizeable leaves
On the trees, the stones which were lacking
A scent I could rest my mind upon.
I went to Exeter; my thoughts there
Were extended by the Haldon ridge
Like a pleasurable stretch after sleep.
Oxford for students in Oxfordshire.
For Devon - how can they justify it?
The great, unrecognizeable leaves
And the stones which give no peace of mind.
Had I been any other species
Of creature, I should have had rights groups
Protesting about my removal
Out of my natural habitat,
Breaking locks on the college's gates
At dead of night to free me. Human,
I've only me, extracting myself
From the bars of a cruel tradition.

Christmas

Wandering wind
Finds a tongue
Where it lodges
In caroling lung.

Mizzling rain
That muffled hills
Sings aloud
In swirling rills.

Holly cut
In daylight's gloom
Bleeds its brilliance
Round the room.

Christ's birthday
At dead of winter
Still relates
What all are kin to.

A Prayer

Oh.
The black green of holly
Like bile
Burns with a thousand red fiery points of pain
To the eye that looks on the
Winter of its disillusion.
Again and again
I say to myself 'Be calm,
Something will happen, some new start
Is possible. Be patient.'
But outside it is bleak and cold
Like an echo of what we call the heart.
My hope is growing old,
And may not be what I call it either.
The robin we term jolly
May be suffering even so.
Neither
What we think nor what we do
Is as it seems
And faith
In anything skates
On the thin ice of fast-receding dreams
To one who waits.
God, I pray you
Give me strength
At length -
There is much to do.

On a School Bus Driver from the Community

Just after half-past three on afternoons
When my young daughter was her father's charge
You drove towards us as we sat together
Kicking our heels against the milk-churn stand -
My arm outstretched to stop her falling off -
And smiled, you always smiled, just as
You turned the wheel to miss us by a yard.
Then we'd leap down, she held at shoulder height,
To watch her schoolboy brother stepping out
Sent on his way by enigmatic words:
Remnants of something going on inside
Which you knew all about, but had me guessing.
What I remember most's your smile, and how
It seemed to hint the same impervious sense
Of intimate conspiracy, as if
The children on the bus were so at ease
With you that things were passing back and forth
Which haven't passed of late between an adult
And children's secret worlds. You said 'Hello'
And as you drew away with a swift look
Over your shoulder turned again to them.
I let my daughter chase my distant son
Who gradually returned from somewhere else.

Devon

As I was picking up one child, and yelled
To stop the other running into danger,
But tears were streaming from the one I held
And the other would not stop, a stranger
Leapt from the hedge,
Stood
There by the edge
Of the field, tall as a house,
With one hand up and a finger at her lips
Gesturing both: 'Be good!'
Quiet as a mouse!
And stillness frozen as a stream ice grips!

'I am Devon' she said.
As I surveyed her granite head
And the red sandstones of her hair
And green eyes glimmering like a wood,
And saw her clothes of town and village
Torn here and there
By the cruel cuts of raiders' pillage
I marvelled I was slow to realise
A suffering outline of so great a size,
Faced with her massive womanhood.

...ctd

'Devon' I addressed her then.
'Who has torn your clothes so viciously?
What instrument has rummaged in their weave and knit
To give them gash and slit
In such a callous fashion, so capriciously?'
'Who would you think,' she said, 'but men?
Those who decide these things, those far away
Who inhabit the Metropolis
Have given the word, which no one can gainsay.
The instrument they use is this:
That I, who once produced and tended,
Must now turn prostitute
To make my living; former ways are ended,
My body's sale is now the only route.'

'Look around,
I once had children, young, like yours,
But mine, on growing, found
Nothing here for them - guided tours
And knick-knack shops
Make a killing out of the past -
Mummies last
But where's the future? then the penny drops.
They go somewhere they can help to build,
North, perhaps, although it's chillier,
But getting chilled
Is preferable to necrophilia.'

I watched the sadness of her concentrate
In the rain-bright brittle glitter of her eyes
And saw woods plummet in them, to a fate
Of nature trails which wardens supervise.
She turned and left, leaping the same hedge
That she had appeared from when she came.
Hair curved down her back like acres ploughed
From the rounded domes of hills to where
They level out; set in it, a clasp
Of black plastic had these words to say:
'I'm a leisure centre, have your fun,
Abandon hope all you who enter.'

She, though, had given me fresh hope:
Her loving smile
Had held the children spell-bound
All the while
She spoke, and when she ceased I found
That once more I could cope.
The fragrance of her tenderness
Lingered among the autumn leaves
Many days, and I would dress
Both children to go out and breathe it
Knowing, as martin flown from eaves,
The first-year martin with no way to learn,
Knows that summer will return,
Devon will have pride and people to bequeath it.

The Soap Shop

Soap Shop, Exeter! you've scoured the filth
And seething muck of exploitation
From trading, shampooed it out of hair,
Washed it from plates and clothes, abluted
Pollution with ecological
Saponins. One and only Soap Shop,
Not in a chain, not even franchised.
Devon business started in Devon
Putting money back into Devon
Serving its people with cleanliness.
Soap Shop, how pure you are! Your products
Are never tested on animals,
No rabbits' eyes are bleared or blistered
As part of your hidden formula
For making women's hair beautiful
(And you were started by a woman!)
Your containers are refillable,
Reducing waste. Big stores, please take note.
The Soap Shop has come to clean you up.
(Though of course some, as a matter of
Principle, don't believe in washing.)
Suds from Soap Shop, back up in the drains
Of Sainsbury and Marks and Spencer,
Of Tesco, Boots, Woolworths and Gateway,
Who have colonised us, made our streets
Resemble everyone else's streets
All over the country, and emptied
Our pockets to benefit their boards
(Though of course some of us will have shares!)

Green Shoes

From the clenched fists of Dartmoor shaking
Themselves at tourists, who colonise
With the camera, subduing life
Under an empire of celluloid,
The river tumbles in white fury
Till it reaches the sea at Totnes
And's lulled with the wild, free pulse of it.
Here, larger than life in overalls,
Stranger than science fiction, being
Heard of as a women's collective,
Five-faced, you decorate your part of
Devon, and get your building ready.
Taller with hair tied up, you're stretching
Towards fulfilment of your most prized
Ambition, as you paint the ceiling
Of what is to be, at last, your own
Workshop. Who can describe the forces
Driving you, the ocean currents,
Deep, hot, and green, which for the most part
Sweep you against ephemeral winds?
The seagull crying on the rooftop
Announces landfall, a rootedness
After the wilderness at sea for
You, who've abandoned ship by spurning
Conventional careers. That vessel,
Steered by the City, is a gun-boat
Which bullies from an alien land.
Bold, beautiful in your small surrounds,
You'll bend to a customer and flush
The colour of red soil, in fitting
Feet with something that allows them still
To feel the earth they have risen from.

s

The Green Man

John Elford, of Sheepstor, initially a Parliamentaria became disillusioned with Oliver Cromwell's methoc the Commonwealth. When news of his disaffection party to be sent to arrest him, Elford hid in a cave Sheepstor, and amused himself by painting pictures walls. The Green Man motif, common on church ro around Dartmoor, was a symbol of that oral, poetic to mediaeval religion which Cromwell wished to sta once and for all.

I dreamt last night I walked to see
John Elford in his cavern;
It was as crammed with company
As pay-night in a tavern.

Yet round him winked not drinking men,
No mugs of liquor bubbled,
But paintings filled the walls, five, ten,
Oh ten and twenty doubled -

Sixty at least, and each a name
From Dartmoor's granite story.
There Childe the Saxon hunter came,
His snow-caked tunic gory;

Beyond him sprawled his murdered horse;
Much good the slaughter did him,
When cold inquired without remorse
Where the slit carcase hid him.

There Francis Drake was ploughing peat
Behind his horse's traces,
And in his track a glassy leat
Reflected stony faces.

Old Crockern stared with sedgy brows
On parliaments of tinners,
And Branscombe's Loaf heard contrite vows
From souls near sold for dinners.

Wolves and bears were wandering round
Where red deer grazed at leisure;
Cows were shown being shut in a pound:
Precautionary measure.

There, in a nook, a Gubbins brood
Was pictured by its hovel,
Ruder than any heroes you'd
Find in a Bronte novel.

There Dewar sealed, at Widecombe Church,
The bargain he was keeping,
Using a storm-light in his search
For Jan, surprised while sleeping.

Another Jan, near Rowbrook Farm,
When summer's air grew dewy,
Was shown about to come to harm
Lured by a phantom 'Coo-ee'.

Other faces of every sort
Were there, both strange and many,
But strangest of the lot, I thought,
And like to life as any,

Was one which overlooked the rest,
High on the cavern's ceiling,
Whose execution, I attest,
Was drawn with deeper feeling;

As though Elford himself had felt
Oak sprouting from his eyeballs
And in his darkest moments smelt
The wood in paper bibles.

Husbandry

It is noon, and heat
Rises from mown grasses,
The smell of the air is sweet,
A slow crow passes.
The fox-gloved hedges
Are parsley-laced at their edges,
A grey cloud blooms
But half the sky is haze,
From the beech spinney's glooms
A blackbird sings one phrase -
The person in the car
Knows nothing of this,
Coming from afar
Doesn't want to miss
The famous beauty spots,
Drives to see the view
Where gather lots
Of other drivers too.
How could the woman know,
Driving past the spinney,
Driving past the linhay,
The bird's phrase was so?
The hay carried and stacked
By those whose minds hid
Things the tourist lacked
In all she did? -
The wind's gentle tongue
Licking the heaving lung,
The labour, and joy maybe,
Of home well arranged,
The fat land like a baby
Waiting to be changed.

Ash Tree

An ash tree climbs against high clouds of fire
And catches heaven's beauty down to earth.
So you, the brilliant flight of my desire,
Are soiled and rooted here by children's birth.
What other force can close the yawning chasm
Plumbing the space between our lives and dreams?
What other duty or enthusiasm
Sews contradictions up and leaves no seams?
The wind is earth-inspired that drives high clouds
Shaping and shining vapours past the hill,
Untouchable though it touches, spreads, crowds,
Imposes pattern on the sky at will.
So love within us, wider than we know,
Drives us about our children to and fro.

Space

The daytime's filled with children, but at night
You sit out on your garden rock alone
And feel the space of darkness, like a sight
Of the sea, mysterious, deep, unknown.
The bluebells stand in the wood, as far blue
As sky that opens over banks of cloud;
An owl floats by as quietly as dawn dew
Fades, while the stream runs suddenly out loud.
Here is Earth speaking then, but not in tongues
Of greenhouse warmth, or strawberry tenderness:
You are not you, but the dark air in your lungs
When you deliver stars a shy address.
You yawn and stretch like a cat, slip inside
To narrow walls with heart and pupils wide.

Faces in Stone

In the sunshine, in the blizzard, in the wet - rock!
As solid as the foundations of Saint Petroc,
The Celtic saint who chose for early Christian rites
Lydford and Harford as their awe-inspiring sites,
Stitched on the hem of Dartmoor. Her brown-purple skirt
Swept the worshippers' minds up from the sweets and dirt
Of domesticity into the flashing clouds:
They could envision spirits strewn in sounding crowds
Played on like Aeolian harps by paws of gale
That God extended, filled with pearls of dancing hail -
The shapes of the granite tors. Before gargoyles were,
Faces in stone gave the blank spirits character.

When the Affection

When the affection of your eye for shape
Translates itself in movements of your hand
And sculpts a figure, I can only gape -
My wonder won't translate, you understand.
There is no way I can express such love;
Even within myself it lies embedded;
The hand that writes this down is but a glove
Of the real hand; the brain it serves, wrong-headed.

The Gyroscope of Things

The quickest-changing colours rend the year
In May, when flame and tawny roar through buds,
And bracken-duffelcoated slopes career
Cardiganed with bluebells, and trackway muds
Catch patched sky in their pools like a glimpsed jay,
And mayflies burst from nymphs to dance and perish,
And new flowers on the banks spend every day
Scents which emotion's fading memories cherish.
Brief though they are, these flashes speak to me
Most: of the moments when the world is stilled
To thought - slow mist-bows of eternity
Soar from the waterfall where life is spilled.
Then pour on, life-forms, dizzy round, round, round
Till, in your gyroscope, my poise is found.

Analogy

A wheeling of clouds towering still
With the earth's rotation, heightening
The landscape to thousands of feet, floats
Motionless in the gyrating poise
Of April's springing, lightening things.
Willow warblers feel the lid of sky
Lifted, and elongate their singing
At the scent of expansion, which is
Not brought about by any decrease,
However, in pressure. Such a day,
Perhaps, by simultaneity
Of its motion with its stillness, gives
The closest analogy we have
For heaven, when breath's held and buds move.

The Common

How can I clear my head of the crowd
That inhabits it, the bustle, row
And impersonality of life
As it is lived ordinarily,
And focus on individuals
At a calm time and a still locus?

I can go up into the wind's fist
And blur my sight, into the thick mist
And lose myself, and hear a clear stream
Gather slowly out of a bog's ooze.
I can enfold the crowd in a wide
Embrace of faith, now that its trees hold
The wood I am looking for, and make
It manageable for common good.

A Sacred Site

Today I went back there, walked into
The old church house, and saw. Ah, church house,
What hopes we had, we three young students
To whom you were let. You were condemned
In those days, and we paid a pittance
On condition that we had no rights.
How our hearts burned those summer twilights
Wandering in the dewy garden
Or watching the town from the roof-top.
Your oldness seemed inviolable,
And we, breathing it in like rose-scent,
Thought only of the future. We grasped
The country from a green advantage
On the copper roof, and planted it
In our dreams: a new Devon and a
New earth. But now that earth lies bleeding,
That beautiful green earth lies bleeding
Under the bulldozer, same as shown
Carving the wrong things out of breccias
At the wrong moment in the vision
One of us brushed on the kitchen wall.
Old, with all its lessons, has vanished:
Old-style is merely imitation,
On the surface, to fleece the tourists
Who are shepherded here by brochures.
Outside, the garden makes a car-park.
Rain keeps on at the mulberry-tree -
The same whose black eyes lured us night-times
To climb and pick her fruit - its bullets
Drumming the crown down, oppressing leaves
Which felt the uplifting laughter once
Of a fountain's play, when we had hopes
And rambled about earth's destiny.
Brentor church on the fringe of Dartmoor
Rode in the sky of the wide mural
Like an anchored and visionary
Vessel over modern Exeter,
Our Beatrice, our passion's symbol,
And the heron that dropped at sunrise
To angle for goldfish in the weed

With priestly stillness, became giant
In our minds as Nature's stately crane
Towering over the building sites
Where the wrong future was going up.
Oh Devon, can it be good for you
That the mural's been painted over
And the church house is now an hotel?

II

From the shadow of a room, the gloom
Of thoughts on the world of the moment,
Step into the light. Here, on the wall,
The past is captured in oil pigments.
Step this way, out of the blue shadow
Of mulberry leaves, into the sun.
Stillness and heat sound in the gentle
Cricket noise of the fountain, and blooms
Of roses look full-throated enough
To have floated out of a blackbird.
Not an escape this, not denial
Of industrial landscape produced
By catering for health and comfort,
But the rediscovery of joy.
Amid the grey of compromises
Essential if the wrongs of the past -
The selfishness and exploitation
Evident in the shortcuts captains
Have taken to improve their corner
At a cost to the rest - essential
If these are to be mitigated,
It is nevertheless essential
Also not to forget the ideal -
The goal towards which, all things being
Equal (and they are not) we would strive.

...ctd

Step this way, step this way, to the light,
To the pool at the heart of the light,
And the open door the fountain veils
Sketchily, as if inviting you,
The fountain ploughing the light, turning
Beams over to uncover gemstones:
Like teeming facets in the wild glass
(Glass that was produced in factories)
Of bow windows drenched in the garden
They catch at as it passes through them.

Tea and Cement

I call to find you underground a floor.
The house is old, the Roman wall runs near.
A workshop when it's finished, but the sheer
Work involved is more than you bargained for.
You go on pointing as before,
Not minding that I stand and watch with tea
And sometimes disagree
With what you are saying. Snicker-snack! your trowel
Slaps cement against the wall
And shapes it like the metaphor
You build to take your meaning. I insist
You throw more light upon that area
And try to give the lamp a twist,
But you, knowing your own house well, are warier
Of how the lamp is fixed than of the dark.
I fear I have overstepped the mark.
You go on pointing, pushing up cement
With your bare hands, moulding now like clay
Into the corners where the instrument
Is clumsy, and you like it anyway.
You go on talking just the same
And if I feel a little awkward, lame,
You don't notice, or if you do,
Don't let it alter things between us two:
The amicable quarrel we rehearse
On the subject of a city we both love,
Which I panegyrise at a remove above
But you build from beneath, and have a right to curse.

Vision at Gorah Rocks

We leave our cars
In a disused field,
Descend the cliff stairs
With shore concealed,
Suddenly revealed.

The waves
Roll, roll, roll;
Foam
Laves, laves, laves
The rock's dome;
Beyond the tiers of surf
Sea glints like chandeliers.
Crash, laughter, crash -
The rhythmic corrugations curl,
Photon-spangled,
Furl, swirl,
Blond and tangled,
Spread head
As children dash -
Crash, laughter, crash -
Chasing the draining comb,
Eyes straining
Against the draw,
And then the roar
Again
Laves, laves, laves
The shoal.

Under the moon's traction
The sea
Beats, knocks, eats
At Gorah Rocks,
Unrolls a lavish dirge
For human agony:
Torn thoughts,
Disease, starvation, pain,
Bereavement, hurled, unfurled
As each wave breaks its back
On the black structure

Of the rolling world.
High on the cliff,
Piped through fracture,
A vein of quartz
Pole-size or less,
Pink, as with the tenderness
Of its sudden molten upsurge,
Shines from the siltstone's aeons
Of slow, inexorable, transformed compaction -
Hope

That the mists of unreality
Will be burnt up from Devon's coastline:
Invisible fog behind the eyes,
Fog on the camping sites, fog wrapping
The barns converted to holiday
Cottages, fog around second homes.
There's no dark child now, met with at dusk
Down the overgrown path, or hanging
About on village corners, who prompts
Exclamations of beauty - the cliffs
And the shorelines have taken its place:
Those lifeless rocks, that compassionless
Inhospitality of the sea.

Hope
That on the site of the full car-park
Glittering like the facetted sea
With new, imported cars, will arise
A factory for car production
Of another era, without waste,
Noislessly, through co-operation
Of makers, on National Trust land,
So that humans may be beautiful:
With utter reality of fear,
With horrible potential of pain
Balanced against the great joy we share.

POETRY, SCIENCE AND COMMUNITY

by Mark Beeson

Anyone who has worked in a modern scientific field and gone on to write up the results of their research will have had the sense of working with a medium - language - which is not tailor-made for the job. Language, as we learn to speak and write it when we are young, is full of unexpected connections: apples are sweet, but so are people; the same name is given to different individuals. Some of the connections are historical fossils: for example the verb 'to steam-roll', meaning to overwhelm completely, derives from the vanished days when steam powered our heavy rollers. Many, though, are the result of everyday experience, prompted by the desire to unify that experience until it becomes manageable. Connections which are beyond the logical significance of a word tend to get in the way of scientific discourse, which is generally concerned with reducing experience into component parts for re-assembly in some more directed fashion, such as the production of technological inventions or the generation of scientific theorems. When using everyday language, the scientist finds that he or she is dealing with words that signify more than is required, having unwanted associations which are foreign to the narrow and specific nature of what is being said; simultaneously the words may not be general enough in their logical force. For example, the verb 'to ape', meaning to imitate, is an unhappy one for the primatologist, whereas to the student of English literature or the child at the zoo it presents no problem.

Faced with such an unruly servant as language, the scientist has two alternatives, if a scientific approach is to be maintained. He or she can choose words from the dictionary which are not everyday, and which therefore are more likely to be associatively neutral, usually derived from Latin or Greek. Using Latin or Greek roots to aid decipherment, new words can be invented. Such words may be completely free of association. Alternatively, he or she can take words from everyday language and sterilise them (knocking most of the associative germs on the head) by redefining them towards the required purpose. Thus an electromagnetic 'field' in physics has almost nothing to do with enclosed land on a farm, and 'ritual' behaviour in zoology has almost nothing to do with religion. This second alternative has the advantage that a little residual meaning from the everyday usage is carried over into the scientific discourse to aid the reader's comprehension, which is useful if the latter does not know Latin or Greek.

Here we come up against a paradox. In order to further advances in a particular discipline most efficiently, the scientist is under pressure to ignore connections with other areas of life, connections to things that are beyond the scientist's knowledge and control. But ultimately such advances are useless to the scientist unless they are communicable, and the only means of communication available is through language, which entails connections in the form of metaphor and analogy.

Hence much use of language for scientific purposes constitutes an unhappy hybrid - an assembly of words with enough acknowledgement of everyday language to convey one layer of meaning, but with little or no attention paid to their associative charge, which is left knocking around, like noise in a signal, to disturb the composure of the sensitive reader. In other words, by separating disciplines off from each other and the everyday world, by pegging out the universe more and more precisely, scientists exclude themselves from communication and meaning, not only as far as others are concerned, but even with regard to their own minds which have been brought up to understand the world in an everyday fashion just like everyone else. You can always make a piece of string stretch if the knot at the other end is giving.

For poets the problem is, or has become, the other way round. For the modern poet, the associative layer in language has become his or her specialist discipline, at the expense of logical meaning. Historical, theological, philosophical and scientific propositions, which used to provide the bedrock of the poetic landscape, are now regarded as belonging to other disciplines, interesting to the poet only insofar as they may spark off an unexpected linguistic connection. But poets too, like scientists, are burdened with the task of communicating, whether with others or with the everyday part of themselves, and are therefore compelled to take some account, albeit unwillingly, of the logical side of language, which has to do with the facts language ordinarily uses.

Let us say that there used to be, and in places still may be, two kinds of language: one kind used everyday in every walk of life, full of the connections and associations which experience encourages and with rhythms that contribute to ease of delivery and understanding; the other kind used for group occasions, for summing up, for drawing together life's threads, the associations of the first kind here more directed, and its rhythms heightened to involve the emotions more consistently. The scientist and poet began by using the second; now they use different versions of the first, which is inadequate for the purpose.

As far as the poet is concerned, the problem of rhythm is the most obvious symptom of this inadequacy. In a poetic climate where the strange idea, the novel image, the surprise connection are of paramount importance, words are chosen in a poem first for their associations, second for making sense, and only third for their rhythm. The fact that words put together always develop some rhythmic status, whether rhythmical, neutral, or awkward, is well on the way to being regarded as a nuisance, instead of the spur to more complete expression that it once was. Regular rhythms that might convey emotion are frowned upon and irregularities, which hinder the physiological response on which the conveying of emotion depends, appear under control only to the extent that they scotch the rhythmical dimension by being neither rhythmical nor awkward. The modern poet's purpose, that of therapeutic linguistic play, is such a small nut, and the sledgehammer employed to crack it, language, is so large in its history and potential, that it is not surprising the poet needs to hold it by the head instead of the handle, thereby suppressing most of its force. A certain numbness of tone, a withdrawal from meaning into statement, is the hallmark of today's poet as much as today's scientist.

What both specialists lack, deny, try to escape from, are compelled to abandon, perhaps even long to return to, is a place in the community. Community these days is a word with many meanings, as any good word should have. The Latin 'communitas', of which community is the English version, has two roots: con- meaning together and mu- meaning to bind. Their combination is the stem from which all other meanings have branched. Community, in so far as the term possesses human potency, has something to do with that group of human beings which is diverse enough to form a microcosm of human experience, and small enough, and with enough common interest, to make use of the experience for the common good. To talk about the scientific community or the literary community is for this reason a deception, because scientists and writers are not diverse in the microcosmic sense - they are all doing more or less the same thing, and depend on others to provide for the rest of their needs. They may go to conferences together by virtue of their interests, but there is no binding, only talking shop and disguised competition. To be in the community, the scientist needs to think not so much about absolute knowledge and grants, but more about: 'Will my experiment help Ms A down the road with her problem, and will it instigate a problem for Mr B up the road, and will it cause suffering to animal C whose mother I gave away as a kitten?' To be in the community, the writer needs to think not so much about style and critics, but more about: 'Will my book help Mr D across the way come to terms with his past? Will it offend Ms E upstairs because I have used her as a model? Will it contribute to the perpetuation of cruelty experienced by animal F which I see in the park every day, because one of my characters' worst term of abuse is to call another person an "animal"?' Here is drawing threads together, here is meaning, here is reconciliation of emotions, all in the making.

It seems nonsensical for either scientists or poets to be using their mediums of communication at half-cock, especially in their most important utterances. No-one feels happy about doing something less than well, or about using a tool - language - that they are not able to extend to its full potential. For both science and poetry, disciplines traditionally concerned with explaining the world to us, a new diction is required, one which makes full use of the associative, logical and rhythmic powers of language (as well as other powers not here touched on). This can only be built up slowly, with many mistakes and much hard labour, by working within the community, confining effort and terms of reference to very small geographical areas over which binding is possible. Otherwise we run the risk of becoming literally meaningless.

GOD AND NEW POETS

by Christopher Southgate

David Daiches' book 'God and the Poets'[1] examines poetic treatment of religious themes from the Book of Job to the visionary poetry of Muir and Macdiarmid. Daiches identifies a creative tension in English poetry between a poet's own religious experience and the implicit Christian faith common to the culture. In the course of the nineteenth century, the intellectual climate having moved a long way towards agnosticism, this creative tension is gradually lost. Assumptions of faith cease to be made (by poet or reader). The poetry becomes solipsistic, over-concerned to relate everything to the poet's own introspective process. Hopkins he quotes as an honourable exception, in that for Hopkins there is always Christ, Christ present and immanent, as a third party in the interaction between poet and reader. He is not there as a credal or cultural assumption, but as a 'given' of Hopkins' own personal faith. This leads the poet to demonstrate that immanence - resolving, reconciling, but always paradoxical - through his understanding of nature and the interaction of the formal structures and every-day idioms. In that sense Hopkins may be regarded as the first 'modern' English Christian poet[2].

The major figure in this new tradition was TS Eliot (1888-1965), and within ten years of his death Eliot's faith must have seemed an eccentricity to most of his readers, such has been the breakdown of common cultural assumptions. This despite every indication of a substantial residual belief in God (at least as judged by the proportion of the population who admit to prayer). Also despite a sense, perhaps particularly strong among those who have abandoned a formal connection with the Church, that our society rests on treasured moral principles inescapably associated with Christianity.

At the end of his book Daiches seeks to understand how the reader may appreciate, and sense great art within, poetry the theology of which is alien or repugnant to his own experience. Indeed, he concludes that a certain theological displacement between poet and reader may possibly be an advantage, provided that the reader is familiar with the sources and images being evoked.

This gives the developing Christian poet two intricately related problems. One is that the biblical stories and images are no longer secure in people's minds. Their introduction may therefore seem arcane, even arbitrary. The other is that of the sheer wealth of this culturally discarded source material - at all costs the poet must avoid mere successions of quotations from Gospels, Psalms, Songs of the Suffering Servant. (Those brought up in Anglicanism have also to contend with the seductions of the Book of Common Prayer; Eliot's own 'Four Quartets' is another 'trap' - one into which I have plunged head first, eyes open, in my 'All Manner of Thing shall be Well').

Mark has written of the limitation of particular forms of language. The Christian poet risks working in a form of language, a symbol-system, from which the majority of people are increasingly isolated. This indeed is the contemporary ethos - belief-systems come to be regarded as essentially private, not matters for debate. The terms of reference of the Christian Gospel are regarded as a) offensive to the status quo (as they have been to every human presumption since the days of St Paul), b) archaic, c) proselytising, d) cliched. A difficult obstacle course to negotiate!

By its very nature poetry is a medium for debate

and exploration - it explores common ground, common territory of lore and image and rhythmic association. If the ancient creeds are excluded, what is the common ground which is taking its place? A fascination with nature persists: this has its roots in the old pantheism, brilliantly but not lastingly subsumed in the Gospel in the work of the Celtic saints. In the distortions of our contemporary society even natural images are losing their potency - even the fruitfulness of the earth is to those who work it an ambiguous blessing. Every aspect of Nature now confronts us with moral dilemmas - she is thus a poor choice for a poet's pantheon.

The other common ground of contemporary poetry is, as Mark suggests, a love of particular attributes of the medium itself. This, I submit, is the reason why modern poetry is almost exclusively read by people who write it. Rarely - with odd exceptions as when Tony Harrison's 'V' hit the headlines, or the name of Irina Ratushinskaya first became known -is it associated in Britain with any of the major elements of public discourse. This in sharp contrast to a country such as the (otherwise-little-to-be-envied) modern Nicaragua.

Poetry, if it is to survive, must not only delight at a technical and associational level, but must derive from the belief-systems of those who write it, and reach down into the beliefs of those who read it.

In our society the most vigorous Christian groups tend to be 'gathered' rather than parochial; they comprise a sub-section of a pluralist community. Within these gathered groups standing away to write poetry may rightly be regarded as of less value than relationship with the God of whom it speaks. And where the faith of the group is perceived as threatened, the tension mentioned above between the poet's experience and the faith he inherits may not be a welcome one.

Outside the gathered group, however, is a wider

community, still roughly familiar with the essential symbols of the faith, but valuing artistic expression more than shared belief. Here the religious poet provides an element of challenge - his prophetic role becomes apparent and his personal experience may be used to enhance or counterpoint the expectations which that challenge induces. The tension of which I spoke originally has returned in a modified form.

It is the nature of Christian faith which makes this possible. If it did not make an exclusive, paradox-ridden claim the challenge would not be effective. It is right to expect modern Christian poets to avoid cliche (unless cliche itself becomes a poetic device, as in some of the songs of that most puzzling member of the genre, Bob Dylan). It is wrong to expect them to ignore Christ's "I am the way and the truth and life; no-one comes to the Father except by me" (John 14.6). Hence we should not be surprised by claims such as Michael Edwards'[3] that the whole structure of literature mimicks the great movements of the Bible - from Fall to Resurrection, Babel to Pentecost. To the Christian poet language and discourse is indeed fallen, but still in its possibilities it points to the creative, sustaining and Incarnate Word of God. Our very word 'inspiration' directs us ultimately back to Genesis 1.2, the mighty wind of God moving over the face of chaos. The Christian poet will give offence, but as his message is a positive one (Christianity being quintessentially a proclamation of hope) this will be far more than offence for offence's sake.

As for the supposedly archaic nature of the Christian claim - the common assertion that this is a 'post-Christian era' - this has not prevented an interesting series of philosophers and scientists from turning recently to Christian apologetic[4]. This trend is well summarised in Professor Keith Ward's _The Turn of the Tide_[5]. Contemporary science, despite the appearance of 'colour' and 'charm' among descriptions of subatomic particles, is isolated by its symbol-system from poetic and theological debate. Ward shows that its isolation is considerably less haughty than thirty years ago. There is a growing recognition that science's symbol-system can make less dramatic truth-claims than were once advanced, and will never meet the needs of the human mind and heart. At the same time many Christian theologians are willing to examine what exactly, in philosophical terms, is the distinctive character of the Christian revelation.

Modern poetry risks irrelevance unless it is prepared to attempt to explore both the richness of the ancient scriptures and the spiritual instincts which all retain from childhood. We should be searching for the new Hopkinses and Cloughs, the new Eliots and Empsons (for poetic attack does trifling damage compared with poetic indifference). We should be expecting of poetry that it address not privatised, isolated existence, but what connects all of us.

Here again the Christian poet has a great gift to give. Christianity is intrinsically the faith of communities. Hence the particular concern of this book with Devon, where Mark and I both live. It is a county where the crises of modern agriculture, modern city-life, and the modern pursuit of leisure are to be found side by side. We are concerned with the growth of vital, sustainable communities within it. The first Christians 'were always together, holding all things in common' [not stuck in front of their televisions, allowing the soaps to dictate their cultural assumptions]. This was a necessary consequence of the second great commandment that they love their neighbour as themselves, and of their call to be the body of Christ (hardly language too arcane or technical for modern verse!).

This fellowship and mutual concern cannot simply be proclaimed from Lambeth and spring to life in

Sheepwash. I believe it must grow in cellular fashion - that where individual communities, however small, respond to their calling they will necessarily attract and stimulate others. We must, therefore. give close attention to the strengths and 'structural sins' inherent in our local area.

Christians in Devon are in **koinōnia** - the Greek word implies holding things in common - also, and just as importantly, with those in Tigre and Teheran and Transkei. But if this is to be more than theoretical theology we must engage with what we can directly influence - more, we must hold in love all who are our neighbours whatever the nature of their faith or unbelief. Their concerns must continually be our concerns. A plausible metaphysic, surely, from which to write in a medium which, we hope, will once again assist people to explore together, and debate great questions new and old.

The basis of this collection is that such poetic exploration must be 'earthed' in concern for wholeness, truth and justice - the attributes of the Kingdom of God - as they are found, or not found, in local communities.

NOTES

1. David Daiches, God and the Poets, Oxford (1984).

2. For a new study of Hopkins and that other enigmatic religious poet of the same era, Arthur Hugh Clough, see Anthony Kenny, God and Two Poets, London (1988).

3. in Towards a Christian Poetics, London (1984).

4. See especially JH Polkinghorne, Science and Providence, London (1989), and A Peacocke, God and the New Biology, London (1986).

5. Keith Ward, The Turn of the Tide, London (1986).

TWENTY-THREE POEMS BY CHRISTOPHER SOUTHGATE

Destination

I use the moor today, ashamedly,
as an antidote
to blind family anger.

I start the long slope of Hameldown
(the far ridge like a line
of scripture, forbidding self-love).

Wind against. A white film dusting
the kists. Deer-sprites
seem to haunt the valley-floors.

The sky is empty, wash-blue, as though
some controlled explosion
had cleared away its debris

leaving only light, and three thorn
trees, absolute
as to sharpness. Suffering.

The snow's striations are intricate,
seem hand-turned;
melt-pools dissolve my eyes.

I find rest in hard ascent, my chaos
left printed in the white,
false summits disregarded.

As I stump down off the hill the snow
drifts after me, erasing
My working. I walk away empty -

begin again today, apparently,
but feel somehow foreknown,
like that new-etched scimitar of moon.

Solstice

from a photograph by Frankie Fraser

Behind a cloud-shaped mountain the Sun
Is hidden. He died last night,
Plunging into the cold temper of Titicaca.
But the women tell her
The bright core lives on -
Writhing and twisting underground
To some eastern lake.
The girl yearns to go there
Once, at least, to see him born.

The temple stands at the tip of the city,
Giant, precise ashlars -
Granite, like her home, but
Arcane, sacred masonry.
She waits with the stones
And her camera.

The light penetrates. She sees it slip
Up the temple steps,
Steady-stepping, effortless
As a Devon dog-fox. The holy stairs
Turn moon-blue and silver. The highest block,
Heatless still after the Andean night,
Shines, smooth-polished,
Raked like the funnel of a liner.

Its moment comes. The winter solstice.
She has her picture. Macchu Picchu.
The Hitching Post of the Sun.
Inca insurance.
The premium, long outstanding:
Four hawsers of gold.

She fumbles with her lens-cover;
Shakes hair out of her face.
Gold strands tangle in the Peruvian dawn.
The picture is not perfect.
The ancient wall at the frame-edge
Is unfocussed - rough-ashlared -
Of an age with this city
But Dartmoor.

She hesitates, loving this other
Strange, high, granite land.
Seduced, like the winter sun,
By the far side of the known world.
Then she walks away, hawsered home;
At Moor Gate
It will be haymaking time.

Crows at a Funeral

Wheeling under laden, pall-coloured cloud
The carrion birds. Seeing them yaw and pitch
And corkscrew across the storm, the day we all
Went to bury Helen, I could not help
Admire persistence in the <u>Corvidae.</u>

They're up in all conditions, and though
We scan the sky for more uplifting symbols
The crows are compulsory. Fair-weather
Soaring hawks, planing ease, are like
The life of adverts for Pernod and jeans -

Lazy, effortless, taloned, and rapacious.
These black banalities mob our soarings,
Turning too quickly outside our grasp,
Slipping away from reprisal, raucously calling
'Decay, decay, and death that gives us life'.

This teeming day, full of tears and weather,
Holds little for hedonists. A caucus of crows
Blusters through our consciousness. We talk
Raucously of resurrections. The certainty
Is deposited in the over-full churchyard.

Our hope, beyond the bitter wind, is in
The Word that made the ravens, arrayed lilies,
Cast crows as reality. Who suffered
To make sense for us of loss, and service,
And of this so sullen, leering, anvil sky.

Totnes - Budget Week '88

The man with the staring eyes has come
From the other side of the world;
He has seen Ethiopia and has the glaze
Of the burnt-out news photographer.
He shows his lover the many letters
He never sent her, gives her the box
He was cheated on in Addis Ababa.

In Totnes he has difficulty walking;
It takes him ten minutes to order tea,
An hour to decipher - her eyes help him -
Invitations to polarity therapy,
Vegan cooking, the Totnes-Africa Link.

The constants are children who cry,
And need blankets and mothers, and possess
The Kingdom. Talking across their ethnic
Head-caps, their cake-squabbles
The man passes over the burned bridge. Tea comes
From Nepal. Tigre fades; the five-year-olds
Walking all day for firewood fade -

We cannot yet grasp - Nigel Lawson
Helps us - our home, our place, as tinderbox -
Tea, and news, and shelter as God-given -
Tigre as the time when the blind see.

Exe Bridges

Swans, sated with circling the concrete
Piers of the road bridges, lumber
Into spring air, follow the river
As though radar-guided, swim the air over
Flood-controls, over frothing weirs
To skid into the reeds by Cowley.

There the Exe is full, snow-charged -
It scours out mud from ragged banks -
Swirtles treetrunks torn from the edge
Of Exmoor. At the city it is domestic;
We cross it by roundabout, cursing
Queues controlled by computer.

Once, the mud-strewn stream sculled
Between Frog Lane and St Thomas's,
A bridge of nineteen arches,
Busy, tinker-thronged, straddling it.
The drovers and their kine forded
Further down, plunging and cursing,

And the raw wind swept their words
Up steep cobbles to the white cathedral,
Pre-eminent, fortress-like on its hill.
Six arches of the old bridge survive -
Under it we sell each other
Crack, and pornographic videos.

The Exe, though tamed, is still flux
And season. Adam has still the free will
To turn away from his sustainer.
The swans, least changed of all,
Are symbols of grace - with strength
Of wing to break a man's arm.

Symbols of grace, and brokenness,
Are what we need, for the new sins
(All old) that Exeter invents.
Or the vision to recharge old streams,
To see anew, this early Eastertide,
Newly-cleaned, flawed, dependent Peter

Raised high between the heaven-seeking towers.

Marriages

Streams surge together under the willow's shaft
That marks the cleave's opening, and vie
Each other in hectic, dancing fall.
Reflected in tumult are colours of love, a mist
Of flowering ericas, berries' red
For sacrifice, the great broken tor
Above them solemnity.
                                        On the day we stand
In carnation-spray, eyes as large as cameras.

When the rivers part, at a rowan with a cut
In it that might be lightning, we say we saw
It all coming - that there were bones on the crags
And cracking sounds even then, from rockslides.
We talk intensely now, repair our banks,
Rejoice in common jokes, alluvial silts,
And at night we cling
                                        but as we kiss look past
The other, eyes questing around for lifebelts.

For the Christian students at Dartington College of Arts

Shall we cast our convictions
Like a ball of scrumpled silk
Thrown floating across a stage,
Diaphanous under the harsh arcs?

Or shall we, from a place
Of safety, throw rosebuds that
When we, petal-fleshed,
Pull back, trail blood from thorns?

No, let us stand together,
Clothe each other, and be clothed
In light's whole armour - let us
Wear righteousness' gift.

We shall be blessed, and go hungry;
We shall walk the narrow paths
About the storm-coloured manor;
We shall see angels in the grounds.

The wisdom of serpents shall grow
Among the old trees. Our cast
Shall be the broadcloth
Of truth. We shall hold on.

The Mosaicist

When I was younger I would sometimes boast
In gold, and calculate a grand design.
Now I know I lack that taint, the almost-
Madness of creation, the genius of line.
I colour others' angels, attempt again
The sturdy Tree of Life - consistency
Of halo, hart, and heav'n, technique leaf-thin,
In these must be my petty mastery.
And they have made me teacher now, among
The shining stones, discerner of early talents;
My self-denial, the smile I give the young
As mists of colour stir, is read as balance.
The Lord alone knows patience for a liar
And how I long to see these dusts take fire.

Authenticity

reflections on academic theology

We may reject the reading of the Codex Bezae
And a few contentious papyri - this is surely
Something superposed by the politics
Of the Early Church, and corrupted
By scribal transmission.

It is inconceivable,
On our present understanding,
That a first-century teacher
Could have said this.

Other noteworthy rejected readings
Speak of his anger and his suffering.
With obstinate regularity they talk
Of him as king.

His reputation was swelled by a mystical polemical
Pragmatist, who suffered illusions in Syria.
Of his fourteen letters only seven,
Surely, are authentic, and in them
His philosophy cannot be said to cohere.

We have been given a fund of stories -
Offensive at the time - Samaritan,
Tax-collector, prostitute, Cross -
Which we think we know by heart.

We have three thousand manuscripts to be wise by,
And know the Pharisees for upright men and true.
We may reject the touchstone of our faith;
He gives us leave.

All Manner of Thing Shall be Well

'Your wedding day?
I do hope it goes well -
For richer - at St George's,
Hanover Square,'
And all manner of thing shall be well.

'You must come and see me at my club
We must play squash - we'll dine'.
The confident English cadences.
Scores more years of them to come -
God willing. 'We'll dine. Your son
How old is he now? He played well, I thought,
Off the back foot. On the cello.'

Only adultery, if not well-timed, or
Whiplash, or cancer,
Corrupts the confidence
Whispers of chaos in the rose garden.

Periodically, in foggy unphysical February,
Or bitter November, some squash-player, or son,
Is lowered into the ground.
Friends walk away -
Make a fuss of children - they look so well
Just like their Father, and the music was lovely.

On the Sabbath day the Mattins crowd,
The self-chosen kneel, well and ill,
In pinstripe and in mink, emptying, remembering
Our hurtling collision course with God -

Also other certainties:
The brand of champagne at Lord's,
At Little Gidding the re-lining
Of the tennis court.
The wind of the Lord blows over the garden:
The rose ignites, and smoulders..
All shall be well
And all manner of thing shall be well.

Cobalt Therapy Again Today

Cobalt therapy again today,
After the diagnostic technetate.
Shares in isotopes rise -
Her red count drops.
Her hair falls out - it
Was expected.

Nothing is expected of the treatment;
These are secondaries. She stays,
Too cheerful to bear for long,
With the priest.
She would have liked
To have seen a healer.

But this is resisted.
Gamma sources must have their turn.
Only when those fail
Will they re-label her,
Give her the glamour and nepenthe
Of terminal care.

On retreat, in the sandstone light
Of a Saxon chapel, we pray for her,
Taking the roof off our lives -
Letting her down inside us.
The intensity shocks.
We tremble as the rays hit.

Who then is holding whom
On the stretcher?
The door swings open
Between light and light.
We cannot look. She is too weak
To unfasten her shoes.

The many doors
Of our castles
Swing open in sympathy.
We are irradiated, room by room,
Our favourite cankers
Targets now.

We would rather have had the drugs.
We long for her to dance again.
We long for death, to take away the weight of glory.

Slipcatchers

Jane is ill enough now to be firmly labelled
Dying. We speak the forbidden word, but
Living would be more accurate
For every day has a different quality.

There are two boys. At their age
I fielded slip for a school eleven -
An alarming promotion. The space
Of possibility seemed vast, my arms leaden.

Now I am part of the care team
Who chatter at Jane, keeping up
Our spirits, and break off
To prognosticate for God.

We talk little now of healing.
The future is narrow-waisted,
Like an hour-glass. We begin
To look past the constriction.

The boys become our focus, and we
Unwilling slipcatchers,
Poised in a cordon, waiting for them
To fly from the involuntary edge,

Uncertain if the deflection
Will be fine and fast, or slow, looping,
The grief hard to sight
Against the light
Of the forbidden city.

Seeing

'See the deer?
See the shape of the valley?
See that bird?
Aquila chrysaetos, immature,
Note the white tail-markings.
We'll stop at the waterfall -
Eas Coul Aluinn -
You'll see the thrust plane in the red sandstone.'

I see the deer on the skyline
And the glaciation, as directed,
But when I see the eagle
My heart, impulsive, immature
Flies out to him
And when we stop by the waterfall
I hear the voice of God.
The red rocks resist the thrust of greyness;

Down over them I drift,
And spill, and chatter my way in peace.

The Nuclear Train at Exeter St David's

Through radiant Exeter air, cold,
Glowing air, fogged only by early
Commuters' expensive exhaust-plumes,
Unmarked, unsung, the train
With the waste creeps past.
Unheard, suddenly, is the birdsong that swirled
Above the Exe, as I, half-awake,
Walked to the station, bought bacon buns,
And thought to settle, using the birds as silence.

I do not know, of course, that it was the train.
The truth is probably much longer, and policed,
And sidles by night past sleeping Duryard.
Nuclear trucks are probably black,
Dyed white. Today is a white day
For ticket-buying, discoloured
By the sight of the suspect trucks,
Grey on grey, furtive as the trail
Of stock to Treblinka. (Forty years on
We are still hanging those most
Notably to blame.)

I leave for London,
Where the grey trucks are timetabled.
In black fear I clutch
A white-day 'saver'.

Lincoln Continental

It was the longest, bronzest,
Ugliest car I'd ever seen.
A Lincoln Continental,
Front wheel wedged in a Dartmoor ditch.

Others jeered, but I, curious,
Stopped and sympathised,
Arranged men, hydraulic jacks, bending
Under two tons of steel.

The owner, the king-emperor
Of the two bronze tons
Thrashed around his car,
His magic suddenly no longer potent -
His daughter's Walkman
The only working machinery left him.
A parable of the age to come -
Small, in the end, is not only beautiful
(Like his daughter)
But is all that will survive the disaster.

Empires of all sorts, long, bronze,
Ineffable, ugly, will pass away,
And we'll be priests,
Levites, and thieves,
On the road from Jericho
To Princetown.

Mozart's Requiem in a Village Church

There is some trepidation
In the rural strings
And more in the audience

As they shuffle in, cope
With pillars. Some, well-briefed,
Whisper of Sussmayer.

We begin. The bassoonist, punk, twenty,
Down from London by one-two-five,
Is easy with her part;

Her counterpoint is light -
She is not foxed by Bax
Or ruffled by Duruflé,

But as she plays I see
Her heart fall, Constanza's,
Into the scoring,

Our hearts, alto quavers,
Plaintive bird-cries,
Are overstridden in the bass -

We are all alone
With mortality
And the Agnus Dei.

At last the Requiem
Dies away into
Rook-broken quietness.

Punk and pensioner rest
A moment, at the lych-gate,
Brought together by a death.

Sunset over Exmoor

From the Crown Hotel, Exford,
Where they still have stabling for gentlemen,
We watch the sunset by dint
Of discount vouchers. There almost had
To be a poem there, to justify the bill.
Privilege. Poetry at several pounds a line.
Is it accountability, then,
That draws from me
How those clouds lie
On that western hill
Like quill pens,
Their feather-edges honed
As the sun falls away from them,
Gone to boil the sea beyond Lynmouth?

Or is it love
That gives me eyes and words?
The deer think their way
Up onto the hill, beside the sky,
That same love's
Most generous calligraphy.

Writers' Morning

Blustery air rattles the window-catch
To wake us, surprises me till I remember -
The first day warm enough to open
Windows that were always flung wide
At night in childhood holidays.
And I hear again childhood's first
Summer wood-pigeon, wind through great trees,
First sneeze coming, of new-mown Devon.
This morning then spans time - I think
Of telling you, think better, hold you,
Touch gold at the nape of your neck.
For joy I want to stop time, arrest
The copper beech leaves at their hue
Of new Beaujolais, and the reddish sun at the angle
At which it first catches my neighbour's new thatch.

I do not want to change the status
Of the extreme peace of holding you
Or of the impatience I know is coming;
You'll goad me out of bed and I'll pretend
Not to be glad to make fresh coffee, and take
A fresh white page to stare at.

I savour in advance tiredness -
Filled page, flavour of your newest song -
Violet and indigo after the setting sun.
I dread our 'undoing' epitaph, yet death
Which is also in this moment gives
To every breath before we get to work
Its intensity. In your arms I am child
And widower remembering.

I start to rise, ready to be busy.
You move your fair and tousled head,
Half-sleeping still, call out.
I fall back, time-stopped,
In wonder at the song of you.

For my mother

Cambridge, Ultra, Exeter -
Expertise in Greek philosophy
Abandoned for the care of children.
Not for the three of us, cherished,
At Empedocles' expense,
The old tin scoop in the meal.
Her metal is silver -
Huguenot, straight-chased,
Worn but polished.
Her time the night, when a child
Climbs from her window
To steal down to the river.
Her place the far moor,
Past Scorhill, on horseback,
Her cadences Plato's.
And her note is a long, held cello-note
From the last Bach Suite. Vibrant
On the fifth string, viola-toned.
Her love is that sounding -
Long, chaste, patient,
To Christ's own transcription.

Note: In Seamus Heaney's poem 'Sunlight', dedicated to his mother, the last stanza is : And here is love/like a tinsmith's scoop/sunk past its gleam/in the meal-bin.

The Brown Hawk

Still, on his dead oak stump, he sits, more
Like a Zen master than a brown hawk.

I long for him to fly, but
He is paradoxically idle, this symbol
Imperious. His government
Of the Empire is motionless.
In my garden I scrabble at thistle-roots.

At last he detaches himself from the tree
Sails high, watches the whole valley for game.

My eyes follow, I know
His natural history, his buzzardness,
Intimately, but
My boots sink into the soil:
I am no more hunter
Than a Zen master
Is the sound of the one hand.

Bearing Reality - for Silke Bischof.

Silke Bischof was taken hostage by bank-robbers in August 1988, and appeared in numerous (posed) pictures in the media. She was shot during a police ambush. She was 18.

Step out of role, Silke, don't you go
Playing with men with big guns again.
We cannot bear much of you and him -
Not with our breakfast things - cereal
Just does not go with undiluted
Fear. We would like to be directors -
Call for a cut and hand you cashmere
Sweaters and smiles, and say no more takes
Like that one, Silke dear, you were just
Brilliant. Eyes held the right stillness -
Death in them. I liked the hair, which you
Couldn't brush back - Dieter's gun hand stopped you
(Only his thumb on the hammer kept
You alive - very good, that last touch) -
Your lower lip starting to go forward,
Sobs coming but for now unstated.
Cut of near genius, we'd tell each other,
Safe in the canteen, and you'd smile and shrug.
You are a still, Silke, unsmiling.
We will see gun hand and eyes, lips,
Fair, girlish hair for a long long time
After we throw the newspaper out.
We'll all the while long to run the film
On, to find somewhere in your last hours
Quality, richness of life, even
God perhaps. Nothing presents itself.
No smile. Not even the arched-shouldered
Scream behind that look of steady fear.
Press work gets better and better of course -
Shot good of Dieter, binoculars,
Leather and hammer-clawing hand -
Photographer got all that, and you did not
Turn your head once - at the ambush made
Just enough space to be shot in the heart,
Leaving us that quite still, lovely,
Aspirationless face, remembered
Long past your name, and our thousandth
Debate about evil.

Palimpsest - A Prayer

I have been in your in-tray all my life
Though I did not know it,
And thought I wrote
My own itinerary
In my own alphabet
On the rough, second-grade vellum
You had provided.

I cannot read those old destinations
Now - nor have I love enough
To regret them. I can only peer
Into the bare, summary logia
Running from future to past across
My much-corrupted palimpsest.
Your Aramaic style is good, although
They say you could not write,
And knew no Greek,
And told good stories,
Lived and died them.

Hold up the parchment, Lord,
Scrape the surface clean.
It is scored through and through
With failed love for virtue,
Obscuring the Kingdom's character-set.
Inscribe me a song to sing -
And give me the prodigal's part
I know by heart the song
Of the other brother.

Write in light, Lord,
That I may still read
When my blood cools
Still remember
When my song fails
Still catch sight of you
When I sit to write,
Or share
In breaking bread.

The Holed Stone

Like a displaced moonstone it lies,
Holed rim canted to the sky, letting light through,
Mute, like a terrorist's victim
Holding up a maimed limb in silent complaint.

Usually I show off the Holed Stone
In sunlight, the luminous
Wounded rock after the stone circle
And the lonely clapper (which is like

A tombstone, yet from which
The Wallabrook, flashing
Oil colours off the moor-light,
Rushes into the young Teign).

To climb the Down today was to walk
Into a wall of wind. Not to notice
The rain for blasting, battering,
Until soaked jeans stuck themselves to skin.

I stood on that down as on an Atlantic
Breaker, or a savage Scottish rock-peak,
Dead-reckoned, tacked,
Struck out southwards for the Holed Stone.

Battered, canted, benighted moonstone
Glistened out of the dusk
In the sleeting, vicious Earth-rain.
Like a vision, above the white rage of stream.

On the bank in the darkness I paused.
The leap was foolish, too far,
Too far, how stupid I would look, stuck
In that torrent. I should go home, have tea,

Watch TV. Still the Stone pulled me.
It was not living, just to turn back,
The flood racing by, the wind coaxing, not enough,
To show this off in the sunshine.

At last, shaking, I stood on the stone,
A waterproofed huddle hiding
The hideous entry-wound.
I looked upriver, into the storm's face.

Holding cagoule-cords in my teeth,
Drawing the shelter flat across my cheeks, leaving
A narrow crescent of vision
Below the soaked wool of a pudding hat.

I stared at the Teign. A flood
Such as would move mountains, or pierce
Vulnerable, passive plates of granite
Surged towards and under me. Raw-eyed I looked away.

Below the wound in the stone the water was dark
As Acheron, or Styx. Yet even as I hid
The wind beat and beat on me
Till I was its creature. I have longed
To live my life in such passionate state
Vision narrowed on God,
Inhaling the raging of his Spirit,
The ruach elohenu, but mainly huddle,
Fearful, shocked by it, staring into
The wound God made in himself, letting love through,
His great symbol, eloquent, empty, canted to eternity.

Note : ruach elohenu (Hebrew) - the Spirit of our God